DC

POLICE

STORIES 2

J2B Publishing,
4251 Columbia Park Road,
Pomfret, MD 20675
www.J2BLLC.com
202-557-8097

Cover Design by Mary Barrows Interior Design by Mary Barrows

Cover background image used under license from Shutterstock.com
Photo ID: 393543592 / By alexkich

Book is set in Garamond

ISBN: 978-1-948747-34-9

DC
POLICE
STORIES 2

Lt. Marco F. Kittrell MPDC Retired

J2B Publishing

- THE DEDICATION -

This book is dedicated to all the police officers that have given so much for the safety of us all. To them and their families we salute you for your dedicated service and loyalty to your respective police departments and communities, job well done.

LT. Marco F. Kittrell, MPDC, (Ret)

– ACKNOWLEDGMENTS –

My wife Dorothy motivated me to write DC Police Stories and it was her continued love and belief in me that was the driving force that helped me finish this second book. Without her inspiration and constant drive, this project would not have happened.
To my mom and children, always thinking of you. For without family, you have nothing.

8

Table of Contents

INTRODUCTION

This is my second book outlining some of the police cases that I was associated with. I was always amazed with the actions people took when they were exposed to the many different situations that we as a people are confronted with. After forty-five years in law enforcement, I have learned that we are all human and susceptible to the evils of the world.

Chapter One
THE GOOD CITIZEN
1975

Mrs. Betty Sampson was 80 years old, and had lived in her apartment for forty years. She loved her apartment and the area that she live in. She went to the church across the street from her home and participated in many of the activities in the area. Mrs. Sampson's husband had died three years earlier. She had many grandchildren and three children that checked on her daily. Her life was a joyful one. Everyone knew Mrs. Sampson, checked on her, and even brought her food.

It was Friday night and Mrs. Sampson heard some noise in her hallway. It was a knocking sound. She looked through her door and observed two men breaking into another apartment. They were forcing the lock. After a few minutes, the suspects had entered the home. Mrs. Sampson immediately called the police.

Prior to the police arrival, the suspects exited the apartment, carrying a television. Mrs. Simpson recognized the suspects as people who lived in the area. She knew them as drug users and knew they were known as burglars.

When the police arrived, Mrs. Simpson informed the police of what she had observed. She further stated that she knew where the suspects resided. Further investigation resulted in the police obtaining a search and arrest warrants for the suspects. The suspects were located and the police placed undercover officers watching their home. Within two days they arrived at their home. The police enter the house and arrested them without incident.

Prior to their arrest, the suspects had threatened to harm Mrs. Sampson if she corroborated with the police any further. They had sent a letter and another person had delivered the threats. At the time of the message being delivered, Mrs. Sampson told the suspects to go to hell. They said they knew where she lived.

Mrs. Sampson informed the police of the threats and she was given 24 hour protection prior to the suspect's arrest.

During the trial, Mrs. Sampson identified the suspects as the men that broke into the apartment. They were found guilty and sentence to several years in jail for the burglary and threats against Mrs. Sampson, The police also, discovered several other burglaries that the suspects had committed.

In closing, the judge stated, that if anything happened to Mrs. Sampson, the suspects would be held accountable.

Mrs. Sampson returned to her home and was given a party by her friends the next day. Everyone was very happy that the suspects had been finally arrested and put in jail. They had committed crimes in the area for months and Mrs. Sampson was the only person who took a stand against them. Several citizens for the next few months kept an eye on Mrs. Sampson along with the police.

When I retired in 1995, she was still doing okay and living in the same apartment. One suspect had died while in prison and the other suspect lost an eye after getting into an altercation with another inmate.

Great job Mrs. Sampson and God Bless.

Chapter Two
THE STAKEOUT
1976

It was a rainy day on a Wednesday morning, but I was glad to be at work. I had just returned from a two week vacation and I missed my work. I was 21 years old and full of confidence, I had been exposed to several incidents in the past few years and they made me believe in myself as a police officer. I knew I had many years in front of me as a policeman, but I already felt like I had twenty years on the job. Working in Washington, DC exposed me to many different situations, but I always remembering my oath, which was to serve the community and protect them as well. I was not always an easy job, but I was young and very confident in myself.

While I was on vacation, the city was the victim of many bank robberies. It appeared that the same suspects were committing the armed robberies. One suspect would wait in the getaway vehicle, parked in front of the bank, as the three other suspects would enter the bank with sawed-off shotguns hidden under their coats. They would complete the job in 5 minutes or less. They were very good at their work. They never shot anyone or hurt them because they would enter the bank so fast and complete their task with such ease that hurting people wasn't necessary. We called them the Ghosts because they moved so fast while committing their crimes. We even had a little respect for the way they committed their crimes, but that is another story.

It was winter time, the worst time for bank robberies because everyone wore long coats into the bank. The suspects would enter the bank at separate times, not to bring suspicion on themselves. One would guard the door, one would disarm the guards, and the third would steal the money. They only stole money from no more than three clerks, normally $30,000 or more and made good their escape. The suspects all wore masks, but never the same mask at each robbery. They further, struck fear in all the witness by the way they conducted themselves.

The suspects were hitting one bank a week at different times and in different parts of the city. They were good, but dangerous. Most people who committed these types of crimes were well trained, motivated, and disciplined. They learned their trade by working with other experienced hold-up men and women. They are very dangerous people who normally didn't want to hurt anyone, because they'd get more jail time if arrested. Not all criminals believed in this code, but most did.

The captain enter the roll call room and stated that he was going to establish several stakeout units in order to capture the robbery suspects. I immediately volunteered for the assignment. I wanted to be in the action. I knew it would be only a matter of time before the suspects would be captured.

They all get arrested at the end. Some bank robbers had been known to retire after only a few robberies, but, that was not the norm for most of them. Fast money doesn't last very long and neither do they. This was 1977. It was a good time for bank robberies and yes, there were some people getting killed, not only in Washington, DC but all over America. It was drug attics and people who weren't properly trained by the experienced and older bank robbers that were doing the killing. Yet, they were all criminals and they could hurt or kill if they were placed in a corner or no other options were available. They were people out to make an easy dollar.

Once being selected for the new unit I was very excited. The only issue I had was being assigned to work with Officers Mike Scott and Thomas Johnson. They were good police officers, in that they made many good cases, they just had one problem; they loved to drink while they worked, and I didn't. How they made so many good arrests and got convictions, I never knew. Some police officers had the gift for seeing things that others couldn't, like people who carried firearms on them unlawfully. Or suspects that were wanted for crimes, we called, people with papers on them, a police thing. I wanted to change partners, but, I was the rookie in the group and had no saying in the matter. I just hoped for the best and prepared for the worst.

The captain gave everyone their assignments and we all received training in how to handle ourselves if the hold-up men entered our bank while we were on the stakeout. We were assigned to the Riggs Bank located on the corner of 8th and H Street NW. This bank had been robbed several times in the past 12 months.

A place I didn't want to be with two officers that had a drinking problem. I was not going to allow them to get me hurt, fired or killed, I had 18 years to go before retirement and I was going to make it.

Once we arrived at the bank, I was assigned to the roof with Officer Mike Scott. Since this bank was so large, a fourth officer, William Bell, was also assigned and worked inside with Officer Thomas Johnson. The first three days nothing happen. It was very hard to sit on a roof in cold weather, but we managed. Most important, no one was drinking. I found I was looking for the drinking more than the hold-up men. On the fourth day all hell broke out.

A person walked up to the bank and just didn't look right. Officer Scott said,

"Marco. That is our man. Radio the officers inside the bank. Have them get ready."

I wanted to ask why he felt he was one of the suspects, but I didn't have time, things were going too fast. I followed orders and Officer Johnson radioed back and stated that he agreed with Officer Scott observations.

Within 4 minutes, two other suspects, fitting the description of our hold-men, entered the bank two minutes apart. We observed a vehicle sitting in front of the bank, as if to say he was waiting for someone.

While we all had been trained in how to handle this situation and I was ready, I had no idea what was about to happen. We radioed the other officers inside the bank so we all were on the same game plan. We were directed to wait until the suspects robbed the bank and then we would take them out side. We had also notified other police units to get in place, so we could arrest the suspects, once we had all three in the vehicle. We were going to box them in and take them down; hopefully, without any shooting. How wrong I was.

The fourth officer on the detail, William Bell had one year on the job and probably shouldn't have been there, but, we were short of police officers this day, so Officer Bell got the assignment.

The officer was assigned to work as a cashier teller and was given precise directions on how to perform, if confronted with the suspects. He was to wait until the suspects exited the bank, unless shooting started, then he would protect the employees.

The fourth suspect, later identified as John Smith, approached the casher who was sitting next to Officer Wells. Before John could say anything to the teller, Officer Bell attempted to removed his firearm, believing that a robbery was about to be committed. John observed Officer Bell's maneuver and started firing at Officer Bell with a saw-off shotgun, striking him in the left arm. Officer Bell immediately fell to the floor, unable to get up. John and the other suspect, later identified as Michael Tillman, started slowly, walking backwards to the front door of the bank, pointing their saw-off shotguns and telling all the employees and witness to lie on the floor.

Officer Johnson, who was concealed, had radioed the other officers advising them of the circumstances. He didn't open fire believing that other people would be injured. He was going to follow the original plan; take down the suspects once outside and in the vehicle.

Officers Scott and I, pointing our weapons at the vehicle, from the roof observed the suspects enter their get-away vehicle. By now, other units had approached the scene and several police cars boxed them in and prevented the suspects from leaving. They were ordered to throw out their weapons and surrender. Astonishingly, all four suspects followed the directions and surrendered without further incident.

Officer Bell was transported to the hospital, treated, and recovered from his wounds.

All the suspects were found guilty of several crimes and sentenced to 40 years. Later investigation revealed that they had committed approximately 10 bank robberies in the Washington area.

A lot was learned that day. You can't always judge people for their prior mistakes. Officer Scott and Johnson were known to drink on duty, but on that day their performance were excellent and they acted like the senior officers that they were. Officer Wells learned to follow orders and not overact, people can get killed. It was a good day, because, we all went home to our families. Thank you God!

Chapter Three
A GOOD OFFICER GONE BAD
1976

Officer Joe Green was a good police officer. He had been a police officer for five years. He made many good cases and was respected by judges and attorneys on both sides. He was married to a wonderful lady and had four children. From the outside looking in, they appeared to be happy and very much in love. But, appearances can be misleading.

It wasn't known, that Officer Green and his wife, who I will call Sally, were having problems, serious issues. They were having many arguments at home, but not in front of their children. They both loved their children and safeguarded them from their problems

The couple was at a police department Christmas party and appeared to have a good time. As they were leaving the event, the couple started arguing. Everyone was so surprise to see them arguing. They couldn't believe what they were observing. Officer Green and his wife were saying things like,

"I hate you. I will never live with you again. Why don't you just leave?"

Several off-duty police officers had to intervene to calm the couple down. The women removed Sally and took her into the women's rest room.

Officer Green told the other officers that he was leaving and didn't need any help.

Not knowing what the future held, I wish we would have stopped him. Maybe we could have stopped the events that were about to unfold. That night still stays with me. Whenever I am confronted with any incident that is similar to those events, I always go the extra mile to help. It might save someone's life.

Sally told the women that are with her, that she is going to leave her husband. She can't take any more abuse or disrespect. The sad thing is that she stilled loved her husband, but he needed help. He refused to see a doctor to address his demons. She further stated that her husband brought the job home too many nights and would drink every night until he fell asleep.

The women couldn't believe what they were hearing. This wasn't the man, they had known over the past few years. Sally started to cry and said that Joe never hurt the children or her. It was just those demons inside him from that fucking job. She said she was going to go home and get her children and leave that crazy fucker. She repeated that she still loved her husband, but couldn't take any more of the drinking.

Sally got out the chair, told the other women that she was ok, and left. The other women tried to stop her, but she refused and didn't want anyone to follow her. Sally drove off and went home. Several people called the house, but no one answered the phone. We all said that they would work it out. This wasn't the first time we had seen a police officer and their spouse have an argument.

We never envisioned what would happen next. If we had, we would have been more forceful in stopping Sally, but we were all very young and assumed they would work it out. How wrong we were.

I went home. Several hours later I received a phone call that I have been unable to forget. The caller informed me that Officer Green shot Sally, one of the children, Sally's uncle, and a police officer. I couldn't believe what I was told. How a man could go so far into the darkness? I was further told that the uncle had died, but the other victims only had minor injuries.

I was further informed that Sally had asked her uncle and also called the police to assist in removing her children and some clothes from the house. Upon arriving at the house, they were confronted by Officer Green, who had been drinking very heavily. He started shouting and said that "no one was taking his children." Officer Green produced his issued weapon and started shooting, striking his wife first, then the uncle, and one of the police officers that were standing next to Sally. Officer Green was shot by the other police officer in the room.

As Officer Green fell to the ground, we believe he accidently shot his 12 year old son in the leg as the child ran into the room.

I couldn't believe what I was hearing. I started blaming myself, because, I was the last one to speak to Officer Green as he was driving away from the party. I even cried for the family.

Officer Green and all the other victims, other than the uncle, recovered from their injuries. Officer Green was sentenced to 30 years and did 30 years for his crimes. Sally remarried and relocated her family.

I saw Officer Green 35 years after the incident at a policeman's funeral. I walked up to him and before I could say anything, he said, "Kittrell, I am so sorry. I lost everything, most importantly my family. I wish I could, turn back the hands of time, but can't." He walked away saying nothing else. I saw a broken man who looked like he was 100 years old.

This incident made me always go the extra mile when confronted with similar episodes, which I did on many occasions. One person can make a difference in other lives. I still think about the family and how things can go so badly in such a short period time.

Chapter Four
A STRONG WOMAN
1976

Mrs. Wanda Springs was only 45 years old and she experienced enough violence in her family to last a life time. She was married, had two sons, and lived in Southeast Washington. Their boys were 14 and 16 years old, were doing great and everything in their life appeared to be going well.

It was Friday night and Mr. Springs was working his part time job. He drove a taxi cab at night to save money for the kid's collage fund. Mr. Springs always said that one of his main goals in life was to see his sons graduate from college because he wasn't able to attend. The Springs' wanted to see their children have a better life than they did. They didn't have a bad childhood; they just wanted what America could offer to their family.

Mr. Springs picked up two young men at the corner of 14th and T Street, Northwest. The young men appeared to be average citizens and didn't do anything to cause Mr. Springs to be suspicious of them. They were both wearing suits and carrying brief cases. Mr. Springs had been driving cab for several years and could read people very well. He had never been robbed or involved in a car accident. That was about to change.

Once they reached their destination, Mr. Springs turned around to collect his fee. Both suspects pulled out a hand gun and for no known reason fired their weapons, striking Mr. Springs in the chest, killing him immediately. They then stole $100 and exited the cab.

The reports of several witnesses and evidence collected from the cab allowed police to locate and arrest the two suspects. They were found guilty and sentenced to life imprisonment. The suspects were also found guilty of several other robberies and one other homicide. The homicide was a year old, but the firearms recovered from the suspects were matched to evidence recovered from that crime scene. The suspects were both 22 years old.

When the officers went to Mrs. Springs home to tell her that her husband had been killed, she opened the front door, looked at the officers, and said, "What happened to my husband?" and immediately started crying. The officers, including myself, asked if we could please come in. Mrs. Springs again asked, "Where is my husband?" As we entered her home and are about to tell Mrs. Springs the bad news, their two sons entered the house and immediately ask, "Where is their dad?"

We told the family the bad news. The family fell to the floor holding each other and crying. It was one of the most poignant events that I had ever seen. I looked up and saw a portrait of the family hanging over the fireplace. The date on the photo was only a week old. It was a very large, but sad funeral.

A year later, Mrs. Springs' sons were driving home from an evening event. As they were about to make a turn at an intersection, a women, who was intoxicated, ran a red light, striking the boy's vehicle. It caused them to run into a tree killing the two young men instantly. The woman that was driving the other vehicle was not injured. It has always amazed me that when incidents of this nature occur, usually the intoxicated persons are not injured. Their victims, however, in most cases, are severely injured.

Once again, the police had to go to Mrs. Springs home and tell her that someone in her family had died. This time it is her children and not one but both of them. The officers knocked on the door and Mrs. Springs looked through the bay window and just started crying. The officers said that it was the worse time in their life, in that they knew her husband had been killed a year earlier. Mrs. Springs finally opened the door saying,

"Please don't tell me that something happened to my children. I look at your faces and can tell something is wrong. I just can't take no more of this."

The officers entered the house and once on the sofa one of the officers held Mrs. Springs and told her that her children had been killed in a car accident. Mrs. Springs fell to the floor, apparently fainted.

The officers resuscitate Mrs. Springs and call an ambulance which transports her to the hospital where she recovers.

After her son's funeral, Mrs. Springs threw herself into her church. She dedicated her life to helping children who are attempting to reach collage. She helps many students and raised thousands of dollars to support the student's goals. She receives many awards and always thanks God, her family, and friends for their support.

I drove by Mrs. Springs' home years later. I was about to entire and for some reason, I wanted to say goodbye. I observed Mrs. Springs talking to three young men in front of her house. I told her I was about to retire and I was so amazed at the work that she has completed. She smiled and said, "Lt. Kittrell, have a good life and thanks for all that you did." This made me feel good, but it was Mrs. Springs who deserves the credit for enduring all that pain that one person could experience in such a short time.

The three young men were about to go to college and they wanted to thank Mrs. Springs for her support and constant encouragement to do better.

I drove off saying to myself that she is a strong woman and there is a God. She never gave up, spent her time helping other people, and never complained about anything. I don't know how she did it. She even motivated me by her bravery. Never gave up and never blamed anyone for the terrible loss in her life. I don't even remember Mrs. Springs saying anything bad about the people who took her family from her.

Mrs. Springs passed in 2010. She is now with her family once again. I was sad that I was unable to attend the funeral, but I learned of her passing after the fact. She was a great lady with a beautiful family. Her courage never made the papers. God bless to them all.

Chapter Five
THE ROBBERY AT THE RESTAURANT
1977

It was 12:00 AM and the restaurant was about to close. Three young people plus the manager were working. It was a normal night and it had been very busy. Nothing unusual other than the normal homeless people coming in to pick up some food. The owner always fed them at closing time. Everyone in the area knew this.

As the owner was about to close the front door, three men entered dress as homeless people. The owner knew the people as prior customers, therefore he didn't expect trouble. However, profession hold-up men never rob a business before surveilling the location. You can make too many mistakes, if you don't. These men were not professionals.

When the owner locked the door, suspect No.1 took out a pistol and struck the owner on the head, knocking him down and unconscious. The two other suspects also produced firearms and jumped over the front counter. They ordering all the employees into a closet and then locked the door.

The suspects then started stealing the cash from the cash register. As they are about to leave, one of the suspects heard one of the employees talking on a phone. Suspect No. 1 told the other suspects to, "take care of that." They went back to the closet, opened the door, and for no apparent reason started shooting the employees. Each was shot three times, killing them instantly. The suspect then removed the keys from the owner, unlocked the door, and left.

A few minutes' later police arrived at the terrible scene. They immediately attended to the owner while the other officers searched the restaurant. They came upon the deadly scene and find three young people in the closet lying on the floor. After a quick examination, they learned that they were all deceased. An ambulance had been requested and on their arrival confirmed that they had expired.

By this time, the owner had recovered and told his horrible story. He started crying, saying, "it was his fault for their death. How could monsters do such a thing?"

The owner went on to say that he had just installed cameras in the restaurant and we should be able to see everything. In that the equipment had just been installed, the suspects were unaware of the installation.

It was the first time that I had seen someone actually murdered on video. I couldn't believe my eyes. I was very disturbed. It was a terrible scene seeing three young people slain, for a few dollars. The suspects only collected $500 from the cash register.

The video and other evidence collected identified the suspects. The suspects were heavy drug users and had committed several arm robberies in the area in the past few months. This was their first and last murder while committing robberies. They were arrested without incident within a week.

When we learned of their whereabouts, we retained a search and arrest warrant and executed the same. The house looked like a heroin shooting gallery. There were about 20 people in the house. Everyone in the house was intoxicated from using heroin. All of them looking like they were in another time zone. They didn't even know that we were policemen. I have seen many drug houses in my career, but, this was the worse.

When questioned about the shooting, the suspects couldn't remember shooting the employees. When they were arrested, they were so intoxicated from using drugs, they couldn't stand up.

Even today, I can remember so clearly the faces of the young people looking at men, as if to say,

"Why did you shoot us? We were just trying to make money for college."

I said a prayer for them and asked God to get me through these last years. I still loved my job; just some of the things that you had to deal with made it hard. That is why I always said, it takes a certain person to be a policemen. Everyone can't do the job. I have seen this in too many people.

Chapter Six
THE LIQUOR STORE ROBBERY
1977

Mr. Thompson was 75 years and owned a liquor store located on Naylor Road, Southeast. He and his wife had owned the store for twenty years. They had been married for fifty years. They had only one son, who also, worked in the store. They were a loving family and respected in the area. They were planning their retirement and training their son to take over the business.

They had been telling all their customers that they would be leaving soon, but would miss everyone. They were great people and loved the area. Whenever I entered the store, they would always say,

"Hello Officer Kittrell. How is the family?"

They reminded me of my grandparents. Astonishingly, their store had never been robbed or the victim of any type of crime. The Thompsons would give food and anything else to people who requested help. In most cases, the people would always repay the Thompsons later.

One Friday evening as the Thompsons were about to close the store, two young men entered and asked for two beers. As Mr. Thompson reached for the beers, the two suspects produced handguns and demanded money. Mrs. Thompson immediately told the suspects that they should be a shame of themselves. One of the suspects struck Mrs. Thompson to the face with the pistol, knocking her down to the floor. Their son ran to assist his mother and was shot in the chest by the same suspect. He fell to the ground and would later die from the injury. Seeing this, Mr. Thompson said,

"You will not kill my family."

Suspect No 2 then shot Mr. Thompson in the head, killing him instantly. The suspects then ran out the front door without taking any cash.

As the suspects were leaving the scene, several witnesses observed them and called the police. When the police arrived they observed a gruesome sight; two people decease and one senior citizen extremely injured.

As the police and medics attend to Mrs. Thompson, she appears to be in shock and not able to answer any questions. She kept looking at the police, asking, "Where is her family?" She later learns that her family has been killed and she starts crying and calling out their names.

The detectives started working the case immediately, in that witnesses were able to describe the suspects. This was one of a few cases where there were many people were willing to come forward and provide information. By the end of the night, the suspects had been identified. The suspects were two brothers known to the police community as hold-up men.

By 2:00AM, we learned of their location. They lived only a few blocks from the crime scene. Search and arrest warrants were obtained. The police entered the house without incident. The brothers were asleep and unaware that a police unit that had entered the premise. The SWAT team along with the detectives executed the warrant like the professionals that they were. The guns used by the suspects were recovered from the premises.

During the interrogating, both suspects confessed to the awful crimes. They both even started crying, saying that they were sorry for the shooting. One detective said,

"It is too late. Two men lost their family and a wife's life has been destroyed."

I learned of the incident the next day, when I returned to work. I was horrified. I couldn't believe that someone would want to hurt the Thompson family. They loved the area and were always willing to help others.

The suspects were convicted for their crimes and sentenced to life. Mrs. Thompson recovered from her injuries, sold the store, and relocated to Florida.

Chapter Seven
THE KIDNAPPING
1977

It was a perfect day in August and everything was alright in the world with me. I was walking a beat in the 2700 block of Martin Luther king Avenue, Southeast. It was approximately 2:30 PM and a very quiet day. I said to myself,

"I can't believe that I would be getting off on time. It must be my lucky day."

How wrong I would be in a few minutes. I was about to be confronted with an unusual case.

I walked into one of the grocery stores in the area. As I was about to pay for my items, I see two little girls in front of me. One of the children is 13 and her name was Karen. The other child's name was Jean and she was seven years old. I noticed that Karen was holding Jean's hand really tight and Jean appeared that she was about to cry. Karen then told Jean,

"You will not cry. You aren't a baby. Now be quiet."

That was when my police training kicked in.

The Metropolitan Police Department offered its members good training. When I graduated from the academy I felt that I was prepared for anything. One of the courses they offered was recognizing child abuse and this fit the profile. I wasn't a doctor but I had seen several cases before. I always hated these types of cases, dealing with children that are being abused. It takes a lot out of you. I always made me think about my children. How can anyone hurt a child? I had been given an opportunity to work in the Child Abuse Unit and I turned it down.

I watched the children for a few more minutes in order to establish probable cause, which is needed for an arrest. It was at that time that Jean turned around and looked at me as if to say, "Please help me."

I stopped the children and before I could say anything, Karen says,

"What the Fuck do you want?"

I told Karen that wasn't the proper language for a child to use. I further asked her how the children were related. Karen tells Jean not to say anything. Jean starts crying and Karen pulls her farther away from me.

I immediately requested assistance in order to transport the children to the police district for further investigation. Karen pushed Jean to the floor and attempted to run away. I grabbed Karen and she started cursing me and said she was the devil. The other police units arrived on the scene, we subdued Karen, and we transported the children to the police district.

A short time later, we received information that a report has been submitted, indicating a little girl, fitting the description of Jean, was missing. We contacted the parents and they responded to the police district and identified Jean as their child. When the parents entered the office, Jean ran to them, crying and said,

"Mommy and Daddy, she hurt me and said she was going to kill me."

The parents grabbed their child and started crying.

We continued the investigation and learned that Karen was scheduled to be admitted to a hospital the day before and she had run away from her home, but the parents didn't report the matter to the police. Karen's parents were notified and responded to the police district. After consulting with a doctor, Karen was admitted to a hospital for observation. The case was later presented to a judge and Karen was admitted to another hospital to address her illness.

This was another day that I didn't get off on time, due to my job, which I enjoyed very much. This was one time when I earned my pay and felt good about myself. No awards, no good job by my supervisors, but I felt like I made a difference. I may have saved a life and that made me feel very good about my job and everything else around me. My training had paid off and I said to myself, "those guys in the Training Division knew what they were doing." I never made fun of them again, smile.

Chapter Eight
THE BIG FIGHT
1977

It was Saturday night and we were very busy responding to police calls. Every time I cleared one assignment, I was given another one. I use to call it the full moon effect. Whenever the moon was full, all hell broke out. People would fight and get into car accidents. Interestingly, not much crime, just people going at each other. It was the most unusual thing anyone could see.

We had one assignment for the bar fight on Alabama Avenue. It was a bar that was patronized by motorcycle gangs. Everyone has a place to drink and this was the bar for the bikers. Furthermore, bikers love to fight the police and weren't afraid of the police. Many officers had been hurt at this bar and tonight would be one call that I would not forget.

When I arrived on the scene, there were several officers already there. They were waiting until we had sufficient numbers to address the issue. I counted 20 motor bikes in front of the club and we had 13 officers present to address the issue. We were hoping that once the bikers observed our numbers that would discourage them. How wrong we would be. People were running out screaming and I could hear them breaking up items in the club.

Sergeant Monroe was on the scene and in charge. He was a good leader and always thought of his officer's well-being. He informed the officers that we were going in and resolving this issue.

We walked into the club and observed bikers throwing bottles at the owner and threatening to kill him. They had also made the dancers continue dancing on the stage, until they told them to stop. Before we could say anything, one of the bikers threw a bottle at the Sergeant, striking him to the head, causing him to bleed severely. We pulled him back behind the police line and the fight was on.

I was in the front line and was the second person to get hit by a bottle. It struck me in the face, but for some reason I wasn't hurt. Normally, glass beer bottles cause serious injuries, but for some reason, I wasn't hurt. I grabbed the person that threw the bottle who happened to be the biggest guy in the room. I thought I was grabbing him, but it turned out to be the opposite. He grabbed me and threw me across the room. But, I wasn't out the fight. As I stated earlier, I was much younger.

I had lost my night stick when I was thrown onto the floor, so I got up and struck the guy that threw me with the only big thing that I could find a chair. The other police officers were doing better than I was. It was one big fight and every man was participating in the struggle in order to subdue the bikers. The sergeant even got back into the fight. He was an old vet from Vietnam and I think pride kept him in the fight.

Even the dancers got into the fight. They weren't too bad either. They knocked down one of the bikers and kicked him several times. I think he was more drunk than hurt, but he didn't get up. That was one for the girls.

I must say it was the biggest fight that I ever participated in as a policeman.

The fight lasted for approximately four minutes. It might not seem long for most people, but ask any police officer and they will say that it is a life time, especially when you don't know the outcome.

Most people don't want to fight policemen, but bikers, look at it as a role of honor. The fight continued until one of the bikers said,

"Police, we give up, you win."

We started placing handcuffs on the bikers and started walking them out to the police wagon. We all looked like road kill, including the bikers. It was one hell of a fight. That was the first time that my shirt was torn almost off. I will say this, the bikers were a match for us, but I felt they weren't really trying to hurt the officers. They just wanted to prove they weren't afraid. It might be hard to explain, but I never felt my life was in danger. It was just another Saturday night fight at the local bar and the police won this one. Thank God! It wasn't easy. It took all of us working as a team. My body still hurts, but I will say this, as a young man, I loved it.

The next morning we all had breakfast together. We all looked like we had been in a fifteen round fight and lost. We laughed and made fun of the sergeant for being the first man injured. The sergeant took it and said he was never out of the fight. He said he was okay, but the big bandage on his head said otherwise. They made fun of me too, saying,

"Kittrell, you looked like Superman flying without a cape".

I said, "I was flying, but never gave up."

We all giggled and said, "What the hell another Saturday Night in the big city."

I really loved my job.

Chapter Nine
THE NUMBERS MAN
1978

There was a gentleman who was well known in the area. He donated money to many causes and went to church every Sunday with his family. His name was Mr. Ronald Wilson and he had three daughters. They owned the largest home in the area which was well kept. Looking outside in, you would think that they were the perfect family. The only issue was that Mr. Wilson was the area's biggest numbers man. He "wrote numbers" as they say. He never had been arrested or had any problem with the police.

When I first started working in the area, the senior police officers identified Mr. Wilson to me. They said that he was the biggest number's man in the city, but no one could ever build a case against him. Many police had tried and always failed. Mr. Wilson had the people behind him, because he always treated them well. As a uniform officer, I knew that I wouldn't have many dealings with Mr. Wilson. It was the Vice Officer's job to handle numbers, drugs, and liquor violations. I would drive by his house while patrolling the area and just wave at him as he sat on the front porch. I would smile and just say, "What the hell, they will get him one day. Somebody always tells on someone; Just a matter of time before they do."

Two months later, we received a radio assignment to Mr. Wilson's home. It was reported that someone had been robbed and shot. An ambulance was on scene when we arrived and the medics were working on Mr. Wilson. He had been shot in the chest. The family was very distraught and everyone was crying.

We interview Mrs. Wilson and she told us her gruesome story. She reported that when the family awakened that morning, three mask men were in their bedroom. There was another masked man in the children's room. All had guns.

The family was ordered to the basement and there they were handcuffed. The masked men started saying, all they wanted was the money and no one would get hurt. If they didn't receive money, everyone will be killed.

Mr. Wilson stated that there was no money in the house and please don't hurt his family. That was when the suspects started hitting and kicking Mr. Wilson. A short time later, the suspects threaten to rape the women if they didn't get the money. Mr. Wilson continued pleading for his family.

One suspect then told the other suspects to take the women into the other room and leave the door open, so Mr. Wilson could observe. They start raping the women. First, they grabbed Mrs. Wilson and were about to tear her clothes off. Mr. Wilson immediately said,

"Please don't hurt my family. I will give you the money. Just stop."

Mr. Wilson directed the suspects to the money. One of the suspects then stated, "You lied to us." and shot Mr. Wilson in the chest. They fled the scene with $5,000.

Someone heard the shot and ran into the house. Once there, they heard the family screaming in the basement. He ran to their location, found a bolt cutter, freed the family, and then called the police and an ambulance. He also started to administer some type of medical attention to Mr. Wilson.

As the suspects exited the house, they entered a vehicle that was parked three blocks away. Prior to driving off they took off their masks. A witness recorded the license plate numbers and a description of the vehicle. The witness further recognized one of the suspects as a person that lived in the area. This information was given to the police.

The police identified the whereabouts of the suspects. A search and arrest warrant was applied for and issued and we entered the house within two hours. The suspects were caught off guard and we entered without incident. The money and guns were recovered. One suspect confessed to the crime and the others denied any knowledge of the incident.

During the trial, they all were convicted due to the evidence recovered and the testimony of the witnesses, including one of the suspects. Mr. Wilson recovered from his injury. The family relocated to North Carolina and Mr. Wilson retired.

Chapter Ten
THE DRUNK DRIVER
1979

Mr. Ted Smith was 40 years old, married, and had two children. He worked for the Federal Government as a printer. He had been employed for 20 years and loved his job. Mr. Smith was a good husband and father. He loved his family very much. He was also taking care of his mother, who lived with him and his family. Everything appeared to be going well in his life, except for one issue.

Mr. Smith loved to drink alcohol. He started drinking very heavily while he was in the Army, serving in Vietnam. Mr. Smith was in several battles and received the Purple Heart twice. Mr. Smith always drank on the weekends. Whenever he came home, he never caused a scene in front of his family; he only went to sleep on the sofa. He never abused his family or others.

One morning after a heavy night of drinking, his wife finally approached Mr. Smith about his drinking problem. She told him that he needed help in order to resolve his issues with drinking. He began telling her about his experiences during the war. He said that he had seen many people killed; women, children, and many solders. He further stated that he had a difficult time dealing with those memories and drinking help him forget the bad times. He then told his wife that he would get help first thing

Monday and please pray for him. He said he loved his wife and children and would never do anything to hurt them willingly.

It was a Friday night and everything was quiet for a Friday. As Mr. Smith was driving home he stopped at a red light on Alabama Avenue, Southeast. While at the light he observed his favorite bar. He then said,

"What the hell, only one more drink."

He drove into the parking lot and remained in the car for 20 minutes, looking at the bar. He then exited the vehicle and went into the bar. He told the bartender to give him his usual drink. It was reported later that he had 5 drinks before he left the bar.

As he was driving home, he ran two red lights, almost, hitting several vehicles. He was only three blocks from home when he fell asleep as the vehicle was going over 50 miles an hour. Mr. Smith then struck a vehicle that was driving in the other direction, in a head-on collision.

Result of the accident was Mr. Smith was unconscious and the driver and passage in the other vehicle were killed. Upon police and ambulance arrival they attempted to revive Mr. Smith, but without success.

He was transported to the hospital where he recovered for a few hours.

When Mrs. Smith arrived at the hospital, she began telling her husband the awful story involving the accident. Mr. Smith started crying and asked for his wife forgiveness for being so weak. He said,

"God will surely punish me for my many sins."

The police were unable to question Mr. Smith, because of his injuries and his inability to speak due to his intoxication. The police returned the next day to further their investigation. On their arrival, they were informed that Mr. Smith had died early that morning. Prior to his death, he admitted to his involvement concerning the accident and asked for forgiveness.

The two other people that were killed in the accident were married and had three children.

This was another sad incident that I experienced during my police career. Useless deaths, caused by an intoxicated person. These types of incidents always caused me some grief, because normally the people that died were always innocent people who worked every day, taking care of their families. The biggest problem was that children were always involved in some manner. Someone lost their father, mother, or husband. It was very difficult to handle sometimes, but we were professionals and had a job to perform and that was the way it was done.

Chapter Eleven
THE ROOKIE LIEUTENANT
1983

I was promoted in1983 to Lieutenant, and I was so excited and proud of my accomplishments. I thanked my family, friends, and especially God for their support. Without it, I wouldn't have made it. I studied every day and didn't go out on the weekends. I was driven by the emotion that was drilled into me by others to make it. I was so emotionally involved, that I slept and dreamed police procedures. I really wanted to make it more than anything else. I never wanted anything more than promotion to Lieutenant. It was everything to me.

The process had drained me of everything, but now it was time to study for captain. This was a whole new ball of wax. The Metropolitan Police Department only promoted approximately 8 captains every two years, but I knew that I could do it. I just had to wait another two years to take the examination. In the meantime it was time to be a lieutenant.

The chief asked me where I wanted to be assigned. I asked if I could be reassigned to the Seventh District. I had spent several years there as a Police Officer and Police Cadet. I had many good memories and it was a good place to prove myself as a Lieutenant. At the time, the Seventh District was one of the most exciting Police Districts in the city because it had large amounts of drug trafficking and the crimes that result from drug abuse by so many citizens, like shootings, robberies, and prostitution. Also, they had a flow of drug users that came into the area to purchase drugs.

When I was a police officer, I used to live in the Seventh District. It was a different place and a great area to have and raise a family. But, when the crack epidemic hit the city and drugs settled in the Seventh District, the area become a wasteland. I observed children, women, young, and old just evaporate into living zombies.

I wanted to address the problem by doing something and this was a place to prove my worth. As a lieutenant, I would be given the resources to address the problems. I was going to make a difference to improve the area. I knew that there were other things to take into consideration, but I knew the game and the process. I wasn't going against the system. I was going to use the system to help.

As a new lieutenant, I had to work with a senior lieutenant for three months. The Seventh District was divided into three sectors. The senior lieutenant was in charge of a sector. My sector had four sergeants and forty police officers assigned. My job was to learn the process of running a sector. I felt that I was able to perform the task, but I had to go through this stage. George Costar was the senior lieutenant in charge. He was a thirty year veteran and I had worked for him as a police officer. I always felt he was a capable lieutenant, but he always went out his way to hurt people. I hoped that was in the past because I was looking for the future. I think he was from a different time in the police history.

During our first month working together, he treated me as a subordinate and not a counterpart. On a few occasions, he even disrespected me in front of the sergeants. He left me out of meetings and important discussions with our superiors. I questioned the lieutenant on every incident as described. He always gave me some unacceptable reason for his actions.

I said to myself that I only had another two months to work with the lieutenant before I would be given my own command. I could get through this.

At the end of my tenure with the lieutenant, I was given my own command and Lieutenant Costar wrote me a very favorable recommendation. I didn't like working with the lieutenant, nor did I respect him and I learned nothing from him, except, not to imitate his actions as a leader. Up until the date that I retired, I always kept the lieutenant in mind, so I wouldn't ever make his mistakes.

I had other good and professional policemen to learn from, which I did. The lieutenant died in 1993 and I attended the funeral. Not many people attended.

Chapter Twelve
THE GRAVE YARD CHASE
1988

Office Wayne Johnson was 21 years old and had always wanted to be a police officer. He was very self-assured in his abilities as an officer. He was also, the first officer to volunteer for any assignment. Officer Johnson always stated that he was going to work for thirty years. This man loved his work; never disobeyed orders, always dedicated to the police department.

Officer Johnson lived in the area of the police district where he worked, so he sometimes took a police radio home so he could monitor police calls. This was not approved by the department, unless you received permission from a supervisor.

Officer Johnson would often appear on police assignments when he was off duty, always saying, "He happened to be in the area." This went on for a few months until a supervisor approached the Officer Johnson and questioned. Not being satisfied with the officer's response, he ordered Johnson not to respond to any other police incidents while off duty, unless he received permission from a police supervisor. The supervisor also learned that Officer Johnson was taking a police radio home and ordered him to stop.

Three months later, Officer Johnson was working the evening shift. For the most part it was a very slow night. But, how fast things change, it is said everything is calm, before the storm, how true I would learn this again, as I have seen so many times in the past and will see in the future.

As Officer Johnson was driving his police vehicle south on South Capitol Street, Southeast, he observed a white truck driving very slowly. The officer recognized the driver as a person that was wanted for an armed robbery that had occurred two weeks prior. I will say this about Officer Johnson; he had a good memory concerning people that were wanted for crimes.

Officer Johnson immediately notified the police dispatcher and initiated a police stop. It was at that time the suspect, who I will call Bill, ran a red light and the chase was on. Officer Johnson informed the dispatcher and other police units that were in the area joined in the chase. The followed Officer Johnson as he continued the pursuit.

The chase didn't last to long, just a few blocks. Bill lost control of his vehicle as he was driving over 100 miles an hour and ran into a tree. The accident knocked Bill unconscious. The officers pulled him from the vehicle, which was demolished. An ambulance was called to the scene. Bill was transported to the hospital, treated, and transported to jail. Bill was later convicted of several crimes and sentence to 10 years for his wrongdoings. Officer Johnson received a police citation for his outstanding work.

One month later, Officer Johnson was involved in another police chase on Martin Luther King Avenue, Southeast. This time it was a foot chase. The officer observed a suspect, who I will call Tom, knock a woman down at a bus stop and take her purse. It was 10:00 PM. As Officer

Johnson gave chase, Tom ran into a cemetery. Tom, not knowing the area, fell into an empty grave, breaking his left leg. Officer Johnson who was very close to Bill also fell in the empty grave breaking his left leg.

Several months later, Officer Johnson retired from the department, his injury too serious to continue his career. The officer cried as he turned in all his police equipment. He really loved being a police officer. He later moved to Florida and became a police dispatcher, married a police officer, had three children and retired again in 1999. Good luck Wayne.

Chapter Thirteen
OFFICER JOYCE TILLMAN
1990

Officer Joyce Tillman was 25 years old and married to a police officer. They had three children. They both came from police families. Both their fathers had retired from the Metropolitan Police Department, Washington, D.C., and they met as a result of their fathers. They fell in love and got married. Their life was perfect; a new house, great careers, and three lovely children. Even today, I have trouble understanding how things could go so badly for Officer Joyce Tillman, when she had been blessed with so many blessing. But, she made her choices.

I was a newly appointed police lieutenant assigned to the Seventh Police District. Office Joyce Tillman was not in my unit, but I knew her family very well, her father and I had worked together several years earlier in my career. He always asked me to look after his daughter, make sure she didn't get into trouble. How soon we would learn that his daughter had many demons hidden inside of her.

I always respected Officer Joyce Tillman because of the way she carried herself, like a person who came from a good family and didn't want to hurt the family or people who believed in her. Not wanting to let anybody down, especially her father, who she loved very much.

The first sign of trouble started on December 25th. The police were called for a big fight between Officer Joyce Tillman and her husband, Officer Terry Tillman at their home. Several people in the area heard the argument and called the police. When the police arrived, they could hear the argument inside the house, but neither the husband nor wife would open the door, in that they were enraged with each other as they were arguing. Fearing for the safety of the occupants, especially the children inside, who were crying, the police officers forced the front door open.

Upon entering the house they observed Terry hitting his wife as she was lying on the floor. Their children were watching and crying and asking their father to stop hitting their mother.

The on-duty police officer immediately pulled Terry away from Joyce and handcuffed him to subdue him. Terry started crying and called his wife several foul names as the children watched.

An ambulance was called to treat Joyce and she was transported to the hospital. She was treated and admitted for her injuries, as they were so serious. Terry was arrested and charged with assaulting his wife. An investigation was started. What the investigation revealed caught everyone off-guard, including me.

As Terry began to tell his story, the investigators couldn't believe what they were hearing. Terry said his wife was selling drugs, protecting drug gang members, and maybe, even committed murder for the drug gangs.

Terry stated that he had noticed his wife was coming home much later than normal and was unable to explain her whereabouts. She received unusual phone calls and would leave the house, not explaining her actions. Money appeared which she couldn't explain. Joyce even stopped attending, family functions, which at one time was very important to her.

Terry further found three firearms hidden in the back yard behind some fire wood. The serial numbers had been removed, just like guns that drug gangs normally use.

Terry hired a private detective to follow his wife, even during her wok. Within two weeks the detective discovered Joyce's secrets. Terry and the detective met at a restaurant in Silver Springs Maryland and there Terry learned the truth about his wife's demons.

The first pictures showed Joyce meeting with men who were known Washington DC area drug dealers. Two years prior, Terry had even arrested two of the men for selling drugs and shooting another man, who was badly injured. The men were found not guilty because, the witness failed to appear in court and testify.

Some pictures showed Joyce kissing one of the drug deals, who I will call Larry. Joyce also, visited Larry's home on several occasions and stayed a few hours. It was later learned that Joyce and Larry attended school together for several years prior to her joining the police force. It was also later learned that Larry was in charge of one of the biggest drug gangs in the area.

Further investigation revealed that Joyce was transporting drugs throughout the city while working on duty. Terry couldn't believe his eyes. His wife, the mother of his three children, a woman that he has known for over 10 years, had so many demons.

Once he had the evidence, Terry went home and confronted his wife with the pictures. Joyce stated that she was leaving her family and moving in with Larry. She also, stated that Terry could keep the kids. Terry stated that he loved his family and didn't mean to hurt them, but after being told by his wife that she was leaving the kids, he just lost control. He struck his wife as the children watched. He stated that action will trouble him for the rest of his life and hoped that God and children could forgive him.

The Metropolitan Police Department Internal Affairs Unit was notified and began their investigation. It turned out that unit had already started an investigation involving Joyce because Larry's home had been watched and Joyce was observed entering Larry's home on many occasions, on and off duty. They also had more damaging information that Joyce had transported possible victims to hidden locations and where they were killed.

Terry's interview produced sufficient evidence for an arrest warrant for Joyce. It was issued and she was arrested the next day as she was about to leave the hospital.

Joyce confessed to all the allegations against her and for participating in a murder. Other warrants were obtained and Larry and all the other members of Larry's Gang, were arrested and found guilty, including for several murders.

The gang members were sentenced to two life terms. Joyce was sentence to thirty years, in that she testified against the drug gang members, especially Larry.

Terry remarried and had two more children. He retired from the police force and both his sons joined the Police Department once they completed college.

Joyce served her sentence and wrote Terry a letter apologizing for her mistakes. She and her children still communicate, especially with her grandchildren.

Chapter Fourteen
THE BAD VICE OFFICER
1990

I was a Lieutenant in charge of a task force that was established to target and destroy drug gangs in Washington, D.C. The unit consisted of experienced and new police officers, FBI Agents, and Internal Revenue Agents. We also, had access to other law enforcement units throughout the local and federal government. They were a great crew of men and women to work with.

I remember once when the District of Columbia ran out of money and police officers lost one week of wages. Everyone was upset and didn't want to work. Most police officers wanted to walk off the job, but they didn't. I walked into the office and told the unit that we had a job to do, people were still selling drugs to our children, and we were going to do our part in stopping them. I let the officers speak their mind. Many were upset and said, "Hell with the city," but after all the conversations the entire unit said, "Let's go." They performed their duties like the men and women I knew they were. I had a great unit.

They all made fun of me for the next few months, but that is a police thing. I knew where their hearts were.

The funny thing about working drug cases is that you work with all kinds of people and sometimes it is very hard to keep people motivated.

Therefore, you must pick good people, knowing that people do change, especially when you work with drug dealers, large amounts of money, prostitutes, and other items related to the drug trade.

As a supervisor, you are always looking for signs of corruption. It can come in many forms and at any time and sometimes from people that you don't expect. You must always investigate every complaint, no matter how outrageous it may seem. Some of my more important cases, originated from some unusual sources. I learned what I already knew that there are some police officers that will commit crimes.

Most police officers are honest, dedicated, loyal people and you can depend on them. But, it only takes one officer to commit a crime and throw a shadow of shame on us all.

I had one police officer that worked for me as an undercover officer. He was a good under man. He could buy drugs from anyone and had made many good cases. Drug dealers are very conning people. Their job is to make money and they don't care who they hurt; children, women, anyone with a buck and as long as there is a dollar to be made.

As a young man, I used to hate drug dealers. They were selling poison to our children. As result of their activities, I saw people and their families destroyed. I always said that drugs were a deadly game. It was easy for people, especially police officers to fall into the trap. The fast money, fast women, and material items were the lure. You had to be very strong, not to fall into the trap. Drug dealers would wave these items of glamour in front of you and see what they could catch. Many times they caught weak people, and on this occasion, they caught someone that I knew.

Officer Marcus King was a man that had a promising career. He threw it away for a life that maybe he thought was better. Sometimes, police officers who commit crimes think they will not get caught. The majority of the time, they are wrong.

In Officer King's case, he felt he knew the system so well that he could outsmart it. These are the officers that always get caught, those that think they are smarter than the system.

Officer King started giving information to a certain drug gang concerning investigations involving them. We noticed that several cases were being foiled, in that every time we served search warrants involving this particular drug gang, we were unable to recover weapons or illegal drugs from the premises. After thirty days, we realized, information was being released.

We established a trap to identify the informant. I am unable to give details on the method that was utilized, but thirty days later we identified Officer King as the informant. He was arrested and when confronted with the evidence, pled guilty. He was sentenced to several years for his crimes. Officer King had also included several family members in his illegal activities. They were all found guilty of the same crimes as Officer King.

This was a sad day for the police department. It always is when one of your own goes bad. I'm still troubled that when, one of your own, starts working for the other side. Fortunately, good police work resulted in Officer King's arrest and the drug gang in question no longer exists. All the members were arrested and sentenced to several years for their crimes.

During the course of the investigation we learned that Officer King had purchased two houses and two vehicles. A large amount of money, drugs, and firearms were recovered from one of the houses. Everything was confiscated and sold at auction.

We also learned that the drug gangs were running card games and that Officer King started gambling and had heavy losses. To pay his debts, he turned to his friends, who he had attended school with, and started his life in crime.

This was another case where someone thought he could out think the system, but, as I stated before, they always get caught in the end. Greed is a very strong power that drives many women and men into corruption.

Chapter Fifteen
THE WILD PARTY
1990

It was Saturday night and I was about to get off for the evening. It was a quiet night and nothing terrible happened during the tour, but it was the summer and something always happened during the summer months. Something did happen and the calm before the storm is a good way to describe it.

I pulled int89o the back of the police station to get some gas. As I was about to park my vehicle, I heard several gun shots behind the police station. It sounded like two drug gangs were fighting again. As this point of my police career, during the 1990's, shootings every day over drugs were the norm.

The phone calls started coming in; Shots fired with people shot, not one, but several people. Later, the police dispatcher reported over thirty phone calls had been received. Several police units were dispatched to the scene. I informed the dispatcher that I was also responding.

As I drove to the scene, I could still hear several shots being fired. It was as if it were a war zone. I couldn't believe what was happing to my city. But, it wasn't just Washington, D.C.; it was the same in all the cities and towns of the country, because of the drug use. It was terrible.

Arriving on the scene, I saw that other police units had already started doing their job. By this time, the shooting had stopped and we now had to clean up the mess. I was about to see the worst crime scene in my career. I have never forgotten the carnage of bodies.

The first body was a young man, that I learned later was only 16 years old, who had been shot several times in the chest. His eyes were still open, as if to say, "What happen to me." He had a Glock in his waistband. He wasn't able to get a shot off.

The second body was lying on some steps. He was 17 years old, had been shot in the head, and his gun was lying next to him a few feet from his left hand. I recognized the young man as one of the area's drug members. They called him, the killer. His name was Billy and he had been suspected of several shootings in the immediate area. I always suspected, that time would catch up to him shortly. I remembered two months earlier, he was on the scene of a shooting and the person had died. When I walked by Billy he said,

"L.T., another unsolved murder. What you think?"

As he smiled, I just walked away.

The third body was in a hallway, laying face down. He had been shot twice in the head. He was 17 years old and part of Billy's gang. They call him Skinny Man. His Glock was found in his hand with his fist around the weapon. I knew that he was suspected of killing two people the previous year. We could never locate any witnesses to testify against Skinny Man. Billy's gang had the complete area in fear. The police would receive phone calls from unknown citizens, asking us to please remove Billy's Gang as they are killing people.

The fourth and last body was found in an apartment. He was 18 years old and had been shot eight times throughout his body. He was known as a hit man for Billy's Gang and had two guns on him, in the waistband. He always walked behind Billy when they were out in public. These guys were very mean people and had been suspected of committing not only murders, but kidnappings and selling large amount of drugs in the community.

Later investigation revealed that Billy was having a party for his gang members. Several members of a rival drug gang had infiltrated the party and when all of Billy's gang members were present, they executed the ones that were known for committing murders.

The rival gang members were located, arrested, and later convicted for the murders. The detectives worked on the case for approximately two weeks, gathering evidence and locating witnesses.

It was a great job by all the law enforcement agencies that assisted in the investigation and prosecution. Most important, citizens were very helpful in bringing the case to a closure.

The two rival gangs were dissolved within a year because, of the community involvement. They had just gotten tired of all the violence and crime that these gangs produced.

When I retired in 1995, the community was still doing well. Go by there now and you see children playing, going to school, senior citizens sitting on the porch, and green grass growing. It makes me feel good, we all made a difference over the years.

Yet, I stilled said a prayer for all the lives that were lost over the years. So many young people who could have made a difference in so many other ways. Time has a way of resolving problems. I hope to not see these problems of past eras recur in the city.

Chapter Sixteen
THE GREAT BAKERY ROBBERY
1991

It was Monday morning and I was working the midnight shift, 12:00 AM to 7:00 AM. It was a quiet morning as normal for Mondays. I was just driving through the area, heading towards the police station. I was planning to prepare my morning reports and call it a day for the books, time towards your retirement.

I was a block away from the station when I heard a police officer requesting help. He and his partner were unable to reach their vehicle. Several people were throwing rocks and other missiles at them.

Several units responded along with me. Upon our arrival, we saw the police vehicle on fire and the two officers barricaded in a building hallway. A crowd of approximately 100 people were attempting to gain access to their location. The officers had barricade themselves and prevented the crowd from gaining access.

We immediately gained control of the scene and recovered the officers from the hallway, without incident. I also observed a truck on fire as well as the police vehicle. I asked who owned the truck. To my surprise, the owner of the vehicle was also hiding inside the hallway with the officers. The officers had grabbed the owner and took him with them when they ran into the hallway.

Once the scene had calmed down, the officers briefed me on the circumstances surrounding the incident. They reported that the owner of the truck was delivering bakery products to the area's bake store. After exiting the vehicle, he failed to remove the vehicle's keys. The vehicle was stocked with pastries and while he was in the store, someone stole the truck.

The police were called and once informed they started canvassing the area for the stolen truck. Surprisingly, they observed the truck within four blocks of the theft. They also observed approximately 50 young people sitting on a wall eating the pastries.

The officers attempted to recover the stolen truck. It was at that time, the young people started throwing rocks at the police. In that they were being bombarded by the missiles, they couldn't reach their vehicle, so they ran into the apartment hallway for safety, taking the truck owner with them.

The crowd rushed the truck and removed the remaining pastries. After which, the crowd set both vehicles on fire, destroying them completely.

The vehicles were recovered and as we were leaving the scene the young people were still sitting on the wall eating the remaining pastries. I even saw several people walking down the street with some of the free samples, waving at the police as we drove by.

The owner of the bakery truck said, "My boss will not believe what happen."

The two officers looked at me and said, "Lieutenant, I wish we would have just left that truck alone."

I just looked at them and smiled, but in my mind I was thinking, "I agree, it would have saved the night." But, they were doing their jobs and these things only happen in the big city.

Go by that area now and you see kids playing, people sitting in the park, and new homes that cost over $500,000. All the old buildings have been taken down. I am glad to see that the area survived. Drugs and crime took the area down, but good people brought it back from the darkness. Good for them. Good will always overtake the bad.

On that Monday night it was hell, but professionalism by the officers controlled the event. They didn't let the event get out of control and no one was hurt or arrested. During those times arresting people wasn't always the way to handle the situation. Sometimes, just returning calm to a situation is a victory.

Chapter Seventeen
A Troubled Friend
1991

In 1993, I had known Lt. Mark King for 20 years. He and I joined the police department together in 1972. Mark came from a well-off family. He had attended private schools and his parents spoiled him as a child. He was his parent's only child and, like most parents with only one child, they indulged his every wish. Maybe this is the reason for his demons that he later described to me during our many talks. I'm not saying that his parent's love is the cause of his down fall, it's just he became who he was because of their love and maybe he wanted more and his parents couldn't give any more attention. Who can say?

When Mark and I first joined the department, we were very attached as friends. We drove to class and work together, dinned together, and even socialized after work. I really liked Mark. He was very bright and he loved life. He was just a little demanding at times in that he never liked to include other people in our relationship. Even as a child, when Mark established friendships, he always told me that he never like groups of people. They made him feel very uncomfortable. That never bothered me, because I was never a group person myself, but I did socialize with other people, more than Mark.

Throughout our career, we made sergeant and lieutenant together, we studied together, and we pushed each other. I really enjoyed those times, but when Mark was promoted to lieutenant, I noticed a change in his demeanor. I observed Mark being very hateful to his wife, especially in public. It seemed like he took great pleasure in disrespecting her. I approached him about his conduct, and all he would say was,

"She will never leave me. She will miss the benefits."

Then he would laugh.

Our friendship started to diminish after the last episode with him and his wife. I just couldn't take the disrespect of a woman by a man who claimed to love his wife.

A year passed and Mark and I rarely spoke. His wife had a miscarriage. Shortly after that she divorced Mark and that was when he really started to decay. I would see him at police events and he really looked bad. He gained weight, looked like he was always intoxicated, and even had a bad odor.

I would attempt to speak to Mark, but he always said he had to go. I said I would give him a week and I would call him and invite him to dinner. I still considered him a friend. I never knew that this would be the last time that I would see my friend.

Two days later, someone called me and told me that Mark was found dead in his home. It appeared that Mark was drinking and smoking in bed, fell off to sleep, and the bed caught fire. Mark died a cruel death. I went to the house the next day and observed that the entire bedroom was destroyed. All I could think about was my friend. Once again, I cried in my career as a police officer.

To my surprise, Mark's ex-wife asked the family if she could plan the funeral. They agreed and it was a beautiful event. She even spoke at it.

Three days later we had dinner together and I asked her where she thought Mark went wrong. She started crying and said, "Marco, he had demons, I will leave it at that." She further said that she had remarried, was pregnant, and very happy. She admitted she still had a little place in her heart for Mark because he was at one time a very good man, but demons are hell always attempting to get in.

I still miss him. He was my friend and had a great future in front of him. I wish he could have finished it. He would have been a great leader, if not for the demons.

Mark's ex-wife had twins and two years later another child and is doing well.

Chapter Eighteen
A CHILD DIED TODAY
1992

Officer Karen Smith was a young and very good officer. She was so proud of her accomplishment, in that she had a child illness that almost stopped her from becoming a police officer. She never talked about the illness. She only said that she was a survivor and a fighter. Officer Smith volunteered at the Children's Hospital on her days off. She loved children, but her illness prevented her from having children. I admired her for her dedication to help other people, especially children.

It was a Saturday morning and Officer Smith received an assignment to respond to an address on Alabama Avenue, Southeast for an unconscious child. I also responded to the address. I had been a Lieutenant for three years.

On our arrival, we saw a large crowd of people in front of the address crying. By this time, an ambulance had arrived on the scene. We all rushed into the house and were met by a 15 year old boy, I will call Timmy, who was crying. He said, "My little brother is upstairs with my parents."

We ran upstairs and see a woman holding a little baby, I will call Tom. I learned later that Tom was 2 years old. The mother and father are both crying, saying,

"Please come back, don't leave us."

The parents were also attempting to resuscitate Tim, with no results. The ambulance crew immediately took over attempting to revive Tim. They had a hard time of it, because the mother wanted to help. We all understood, but, the medics were the professionals

As the medics were attempting to revive Tim, I heard Officer Smith saying a prayer and asking God to please save this child. Both parents started praying and asking God to please save their little boy. I even said a little prayer.

The medics work feverishly on Tom, but after several minutes, one of the medics gave me that look that I have seen to many times in the past twenty years.

We asked the parents to leave the room, in order for the medics to continue their work. The parents didn't want to leave. It took several seconds to convince them to leave the room. The mother said,

"Please let me say with my little boy."

We couldn't let her. We had to do our job. These things may seem cruel, but are necessary. That is why it takes a certain breed of men and women to become police officers and firemen. It is hard sometimes.

The medics told us that the child was dead and we must notify the morgue. Officer Smith started crying. One of the medics clutched the officer and told her that everything would be okay.

Now, we must tell the parents that their child is dead. Officer Smith recovered and asked if she could tell the parents. I think about it for a few seconds and for some unknown reason I said, "Yes." I thought it would make her feel better. She further stated that she was "OK" and she was a "police officer who had a job to do. Now let's get to it." She wiped her face and had the look of a police officer who has a job to perform.

We walked down the stairs and before reaching the living room, we are met by the parents who look right at Officers Smith. Before the officer can say anything, the mother replies with tears in her eyes,

"My child is dead. I know this now."

The father clutches his wife and also starts crying. Officer Smith hugs them both and says,

"I will say a prayer for Tom tonight".

Other police units arrived on the scene and processed the same. Tom was transported to the morgue and later investigation revealed that he had a rare disease that resulted in his death.

Officer Smith and I attended the funeral. As we were leaving, the officer told me that when she was a little girl she had the same illness, but recovered before she was 5 years old. She apologized for her conduct. I immediately told her that it wasn't necessary. I told her I had cried many times and wasn't ashamed. It had made me feel better, every time. Officer Smith married in 1990, adopted three children, and retired as a sergeant in 2010. Great job sergeant, you did a fantastic job. Enjoy your retirement and the grand kids.

Chapter Nineteen
THE HARD WORKING POLICE OFFICER
1992

Officer Mark Jackson was a hard working Police Officer. He had been an officer for twenty years and always reported to work. He loved his job, but most important, he loved making money and had several off-duty businesses. During the month of July, he would sell fireworks and during the warmer months, he had a lawn service. During the remaining months, he and his brother had a moving company and a sanitation service. He was always working. But, he loved being a police officer most of all.

I admired his dedication to working all the time. He always said that he wanted one-million dollars in the bank when he retired. He wanted his family to live a better life than he had. His family was very poor and he never experienced a child's life in that he had to work as a child in order to help support the family. He really hated growing up poor and swore that he would never return to that way of life.

I use to see him report to work very ill. He wanted to save all of his leave for retirement. I don't know how he worked so many hours and so many jobs. I even asked him how long he planned to work this way. He only said, "As long as it takes to get one-million."

It was a Monday and Officer Jackson was working the evening shift. He and another police unit received a radio assignment for a family dispute.

On their arrival, they were met by a woman who wanted to leave her husband but he refuse to let her go. After a few minutes of discussion, the husband allowed his wife to leave. As the police were escorting the wife out the door, the husband grabbed a gun and shot both his wife and Officer Jackson in the back. The other officer on the scene returned fire, striking the husband in the chest, killing him instantly.

Officer Jackson and the wife both recovered from their injuries. But, due to the gravity of Officer Jackson's injuries, he was required to retire on disability. This was something that the officer didn't want. He wanted to work another five years in order to reach his goal. I have never seen an officer so upset about retiring. He tried every avenue that was offered to him, that would allow him to continue working on the force, but to no avail.

Prior to Officer Jackson's retirement, he had to turn in his police service weapon. When I took possession of the weapon and informed Officer Jackson of his non-contact status, he started crying. I have seen this happen on many occasions when an officer is placed on non-contact status. This means that they must turn in their weapon and police identification and can't wear a police uniform. When it happens, other officers have a look about them, as if to say that you are no longer a policeman. It isn't a good feeling, even if you are the police official taking possession of their property. It's a police thing.

Prior to his retirement, Officer Jackson had to work at the police station in plain clothes and he hated it. In his mind he was no longer a police officer. Everyone noticed the change in the officer's attitude. Furthermore, the officer was unable to work any of his off-duty business. I think this worried him the most.

When it was time for him to retire, he didn't want any celebration. He reported to work on his last day and at the end of the shift he just said good bye and started crying. It was a very miserable sight.

Officer Jackson was retired for two months. He woke up one morning, had a meal with the family, and told them that he loved them and wanted nothing but the best for their future. He then got into his vehicle and drove to a park. It was reported that he parked his vehicle by the river and after two hours placed a Glock into his mouth and killed himself.

No one knew the reason. There were many theories, but none were ever proven. I was sad to hear about the officer's death and for his family.

Chapter Twenty
THE HOSPITAL VISIT
1993

This is a story that I always recall when I need a good laugh; not at the people involved, but the things you see as a policeman. I had been a lieutenant for three years and really felt good about myself, everything was going good. Then I get involved in a case that I will always remember.

It was Friday and I was working the day work shift. Everything was quiet and I was planning my vacation. Then I get a call that an off-duty police officer, that I will identify as Mike, and his wife were at home and threats had been made against the wife by the officer. To make things worse, the officer worked for me. There were policemen already on the scene attempting to resolve the issue. In that a police officer was involved, a police supervisor, me, had to respond to the location.

I directed a sergeant to assist me and we responded to the location. On our arrival, I see something that I can't believe. The two on-duty police officers are standing over Mike as he is sitting in a chair in the living room. What was so unusual was that Mike didn't have any cloths on. I immediately ask why Mike was not wearing any garments. The on-duty officers stated that Mike believed that he is wearing garments.

I knew right then that I was dealing with something more than an argument between a husband and his wife. The officers further stated that Mike's wife, I will name Jane, was locked in the bathroom on the second floor and another officer was watching the door. No children were in the house. The kids had run to a friend's house next door, when the argument started. Another officer had located the children and they were okay.

As I approached the bathroom where Mike's wife was hiding, I could hear her praying and asking God to help her husband. I knocked on the door and ask Jane to open the door so we could talk about what was going on.

To my surprise, Jane responded to my request and opened the door. She was crying and looked very upset. Before I could say anything, Jane grabbed me and said to please help her husband as he was very ill. She indicated he never recovered from the Vietnam War and was on medication. He had stopped taking his medication because they made him feel less than a man and now he was going to kill Charlie.

I knew that Mike had been in the war and I loved to hear his stories about the conflict. I also knew Mike had demons, but I never knew that they were that bad.

Jane went on to say that Mike has been off his medication for five days and began to see the enemy in the house. When she tried to talk to him and ask him to please take his medication, he took his garments off and started running throughout the house waving a stick in his hand saying that he was going to kill Charlie, the Vietcong. Jane further stated that we needed to call his doctor.

I then heard the officers that were guarding Mike ask for help with Mike. We ran downstairs and Mike was attempting to leave the house. We had to subdue Mike with handcuffs. Jane was crying and telling us to "please don't hurt him."

Once we subdued Mike, I called the police doctor that was on duty for emergency cases like this one and Mike's doctor. After both doctors spoke to each other, I was directed to transport Mike to a special hospital that address such conditions.

We were able to place a blanket on Mike, because he wouldn't allow us to put any clothes on him. We transported Mike to the special hospital. Once arriving at the hospital, we placed our guns in a lock box, something that I wasn't comfortable with.

Mike was interviewed by several doctors and was given several medications to address his illness. He was then admitted for further observation. We were asked to escort mike to his room.

As we are walking down the hallway, every few feet I heard doors closing behind us, with bars. Mike started talking and asked us not to leave him in the hospital. This wasn't his first visit and he was tired of hospitals. The staff was able to place clothes on Mike, once he was medicated. Mike further asked why he was in the hospital and where were his family and what had he done wrong. He just wanted to go home and rest and be with his family.

I started feeling sorry for Mike, but I knew this was the best place for him. I started remembering his stories and the good police officer that I respected, but I had to do my job.

We approached Mike's room. I saw a patient painting a wall. The problem was that he didn't have a paint brush nor was there any paint. He was just going through the motions. We didn't say anything. We just continued walking.

As we walked away, the patient asked, "How did we like the color?"

I said, "Great."

Mike said, "Lieutenant I don't see any paint. Maybe you should stay and not me."

I just smiled.

As we walk further down the corridor, I observed another man crying. He was saying he wanted to go home and see his mother. Mike looked at me and said there were too many crazy motherfuckers in one place and he didn't need to be here. One of the staff members with us and he advised us not to take what we see so seriously, because the patients were ill. I knew this, but I felt restlessness.

We finally reached Mike's room and wished him the best. I told him that he would be back at work soon, but I didn't really know what to expect from his recovery. I just wanted to say something. May it was the wrong thing to say.

Prior to leaving Mike's corridor, several more patients approached us and asked if we were new patients. The staff member said, "No" asked them to "please go back to your rooms." Another patient asked when they were going to get their Jell-O. It was past 5:00 PM and he wanted to watch his cowboy show while he was eating his Jell-O.

Then someone in the back said,

"Mother Fucker, you are not getting any Jell-O today, now be quiet".

Then all the patients started yelling saying we had fucked it up for everyone. We must be new patients and didn't know the rules and no Jell-O. By this time more staff members had arrived and escorted us out the area.

The Sergeant and I departed the area, retrieved our weapons, and left the hospital. I went back to my office, submitted my report on the incident, and forwarded the same through channels.

After several weeks in the hospital, Mike was released and reunited with his family. They are still together today. Mike retired from the department with full benefits, due to his illness.

When I retired from the department in 1995, Mike and his wife attended the ceremony. I was glad to see him. He told me that he was still on medication and that he and the family were doing great. Their kids were married and he was a grandfather, loving life. He served his country well. Mike died in 2011. I miss listening to his stories about the war.

Marco and Dorothy Kittrell